APR 21

**A+ books**

# POLAR ANIMALS

# PENGUINS

## ARE AWESOME

by Jaclyn Jaycox

Consultant: Greg Breed
Associate Professor of Ecology
Institute of Arctic Biology
University of Alaska, Fairbanks

**PEBBLE**
a capstone imprint

A+ Books are published by Pebble,
1710 Roe Crest Drive, North Mankato, Minnesota 56003
www.mycapstone.com

**Library of Congress Cataloging-in-Publication Data**
Names: Jaycox, Jaclyn, 1983–author.
Title: Penguins Are Awesome / by Jaclyn Jaycox.
Description: North Mankato, Minnesota: an imprint of Pebble, [2020] |
    Series: A+. Polar Animals | Audience: Age 4–8. | Audience: K to Grade 3. |
    Includes bibliographical references and index.
Identifiers: LCCN 2018056757| ISBN 9781977108159 (hardcover) | ISBN
    9781977109958 (paperback) | ISBN 9781977108241 (ebook pdf)
Subjects: LCSH: Penguins—Juvenile literature. | Animals—Polar
    regions—Juvenile literature.
Classification: LCC QL696.S473 J39 2020 | DDC 598.47—dc23
LC record available at https://lccn.loc.gov/2018056757

**Editorial Credits**
Nikki Potts, editor; Kayla Rossow, designer; Morgan Walters, media researcher;
Laura Manthe, production specialist

**Photo Credits**
Alamy: Russell Mountford, spread 16-17; Minden Pictures: Doc White, 15; Shutterstock: Alexey Seafarer, 21, Angela N Perryman, top right 12, ChameleonsEye, 5, evenfh, 26, jlarrumbe, 8, jo Crebbin, 29, Mara008, design element (blue), Mario_Hoppmann, 9, spread 12-13, top 22, MicheleB, 27, Mr.Boy, 7, Nicepen, 4, Oliay, design element (ice window), Patrick Poendl, 23, photosoft, design element (ice), Rich Lindie, 20, Robert Bruce Lilley, spread 10-11, Roger Clark ARPS, bottom left 22, Sergey 402, spread 18-19, Stephen Lew, 25, 28, Tarpan, 14, ValerieVSBN, 6, vladsilver, Cover, 24

All internet sites appearing in back matter were available and accurate when this book was sent to press.

## Note to Parents, Teachers, and Librarians

This Polar Animals book uses full-color photographs and a nonfiction format to introduce the concept of penguins. *Penguins Are Awesome* is designed to be read aloud to a pre-reader or to be read independently by an early reader. Photographs help listeners and early readers understand the text and concepts discussed. The book encourages further learning by including the following sections: Table of Contents, Glossary, Read More, Internet Sites, Critical Thinking Questions, and Index. Early readers may need assistance using these features.

Printed in China.
1671

# TABLE OF CONTENTS

# Swimming Birds

A penguin dives into the icy ocean. It flaps its flippers and speeds through the water. Penguins are amazing swimmers and divers. They spend more time in the water than any other bird.

# Black and White Penguins

Penguins can't fly. They have flippers that help them swim. Their waterproof feathers are black and white.

Some penguins also have yellow, orange, or red coloring. Penguins have short legs. They waddle when they walk. Their bodies are long.

There are 18 different
types of penguins. The
smallest weigh 2 pounds
(0.9 kilograms). They are
14 inches (36 centimeters) tall.

The largest penguins
are almost 4 feet (120 cm)
tall. They can weigh up to
90 pounds (41 kg).

Four types of penguins live in Antarctica. It's the coldest and windiest place on Earth.

Feathers and a thick layer of blubber keep penguins warm. Penguins hunt for food in the water.

On land, penguins waddle, hop, or slide. They move fastest on their stomachs. They slide on the slippery ice. *Zoom!* Their strong toes and claws push them.

# Finding Food

A hungry penguin plunges into the ocean. The penguin spots a tasty fish. *Snatch!* It swallows the fish whole. Penguins hunt krill. They also eat fish and squid. Penguins eat up to 2 pounds (0.9 kg) of food each day.

krill

Penguins dive into the
icy waters to look for food.
Some types of penguins
hunt alone. Others hunt
in groups.

Penguins spend more than half of their lives in the water. They can hold their breath for 20 minutes.

# Family Life

Penguins live in groups.
During mating season, groups
come together. Thousands
of penguins gather at a
nesting spot.

These large groups
are called colonies.
Some are so big, they
can be seen from space!

Some penguins build nests with rocks and feathers. Others don't build nests at all. Many types of penguins lay two eggs at a time. Others lay only one.

The mother and father take turns keeping the egg warm. They also take turns hunting for food. When a chick hatches from the egg, both parents care for it.

A chick is brown or gray and fuzzy. Its feathers are not waterproof. The water is too cold for a chick. The mother and father bring the chick food.

Adult feathers take up to 13 months to grow. Once a penguin has its adult feathers, it can go in the water to hunt.

# Staying Safe

Penguins in Antarctica have no predators on land. But the ocean is full of danger. Leopard seals and killer whales hunt penguins. But a penguin's colors help it hide. From below the water's surface, a penguin's white stomach blends in with the sunlight. If a predator spots it, a penguin zigzags to escape!

leopard seal

Penguins live up to
50 years in the wild. But
their habitat is shrinking.
Climate change is melting
polar ice.

People are catching more and more krill to sell and eat. This leaves less food for penguins.

Penguins are not like
other birds. They can't fly.
But they love to swim!

Birds are found all around the world. Penguins are one of the few that can survive the icy tundra.

# GLOSSARY

**blubber** (BLUH-buhr)—a thick layer of fat under the skin of some animals; blubber keeps animals warm

**climate change** (KLY-muht CHAYNJ)—a significant change in Earth's climate over a period of time

**colony** (KAH-luh-nee)—a place where penguins come together to mate and raise young

**flipper** (FLIP-ur)—one of the broad, flat limbs of an ocean or freshwater animal

**habitat** (HAB-uh-tat)—the natural place and conditions in which a plant or animal lives

**krill** (KRIL)—a small shrimplike animal

**mate** (MATE)—to come together to produce young

**polar** (POH-lur)—having to do with the icy regions around the North or South Pole

**predator** (PRED-uh-tur)—an animal that hunts other animals for food

**squid** (SKWID)—a sea animal with a long, soft body and 10 fingerlike arms used to grasp food

**tundra** (TUHN-druh)—a cold area where trees do not grow; the soil under the ground in the tundra is permanently frozen

**zigzag** (ZIG-zag)—a line or course that moves in short, sharp turns or angles from one side to the other

# READ MORE

Cooper, Sharon Katz. *A Day in the Life of a Penguin: A 4D Book.* A Day in the Life. North Mankato, Minn.: Capstone Press, 2019.

Salomon, David. *Penguins!* Step into Reading. New York: Random House, 2017.

Ward, Finn. *Penguins at the Zoo.* Zoo Animals. New York: Gareth Stevens Publishing, 2016.

# INTERNET SITES

*Easy Science for Kids*
https://easyscienceforkids.com/all-about-penguins/

*DK Find Out, Penguin Facts*
https://www.dkfindout.com/uk/animals-and-nature/birds/penguins/

*National Geographic Kids, Emperor Penguins Profile*
https://kids.nationalgeographic.com/animals/emperor-penguin/#emperor-penguin-group-snow.jpg

# CRITICAL THINKING QUESTIONS

1. Antarctic penguins don't have any predators on land. But they do have some in the ocean. Which animals hunt penguins?

2. Thousands of penguins gather together during mating season. What is this large group of penguins called?

3. Penguins are different from many birds. Can you name some differences?

# INDEX

32